TEACHER TO TEACHER

Crossword Puzzles to accompany

HEATH

DISCOVERING FRENCH

BLANC

Angela P. R. Giannella
The Foote School
New Haven, Connecticut

McDougal Littell
Evanston, Illinois
Boston • Dallas

D.C. Heath and Company
A Division of Houghton Mifflin Company

Copyright © 1997 by D.C. Heath and Company, a Division of Houghton Mifflin Company

Permission to reproduce these pages for classroom use is granted to users of *Discovering French–Blanc.*

Published simultaneously in Canada

Printed in the United States of America

International Standard Book Number: 0-669-44650-5

1 2 3 4 5 6 7 8 9 0 -MZ- 01 00 99 98 97 96

Contents

Introduction

This Crossword Puzzle Book for *Discovering French–Blanc* has been created for easy use by French teachers. It allows them to review the material on a daily basis. The crossword puzzles may be used in class as Quiz-Vocabulary to wrap up the lesson taught that day. They can also be used as part of a test or even for homework.

I have introduced crossword puzzles in my French and Spanish classes at The Foote School this year. From my own experience, students enjoy reviewing with crossword puzzles and they follow the teacher's instructions from day one.

There are many crossword puzzle books in Foreign Language Catalogs. However, this is the only one that matches 100% *Discovering French–Blanc* from D.C. Heath.

Instructions for Teachers:

Some French expressions have 2, 3, or 4 words, that will appear as (2 w.), (3 w.) or (4 w.) next to the clues. If this is the case, the student must trace a double line to show the teacher he/she knows where to separate the words in the expression.

If a French word has an accent , the student is expected to put it in and draw an arrow next to the letter indicating if the accent belongs to the "across"or to the "down" word.

Angela P. R. Giannella
The Foote School, Connecticut

Correlation to *Discovering French–Blanc*

Puzzle No.	Lesson No.	Page No.	Answers for Puzzle	Lesson No.	Page No.
1	Reprise, p. 5	1	1	Reprise, p. 5	47
2	Reprise, p. 13	2	2	Reprise, p. 13	47
3	Reprise, p. 15	3	3	Reprise, p. 15	48
4	Reprise, p. 21	4	4	Reprise, p. 21	48
5	Unité 1: L.1, p. 33	5	5	Unité 1: L.1, p. 33	49
6	Unité 1: L.1, p. 34	6	6	Unité 1: L.1, p. 34	49
7	Unité 1: L.1, p. 34	7	7	Unité 1: L.1, p. 34	50
8	Unité 1: L.1, p. 37	8	8	Unité 1: L.1, p. 37	50
9	Unité 1: L.1, p. 44	9	9	Unité 1: L.1, p. 44	51
10	Unité 1: L.2, p. 46	10	10	Unité 1: L.2, p. 46	51
11	Unité 1: L.2, p. 47 A	11	11	Unité 1: L.2, p. 47 A	52
12	Unité 1: L.2, p. 47 B	12	12	Unité 1: L.2, p. 47 B	52
13	Unité 1: L.2, p. 48	13	13	Unité 1: L.2, p. 48	53
14	Unité 1: L.3, p. 56	14	14	Unité 1: L.3, p. 56	53
15	Unité 1: L.3, p. 58	15	15	Unité 1: L.3, p. 58	54
16	Unité 2: L.5, p. 96	16	16	Unité 2: L.5, p. 96	54
17	Unité 2: L.5, p. 100	17	17	Unité 2: L.5, p. 100	55
18	Unité 2: L.6, p. 106, 109	18	18	Unité 2: L.6, p. 106, 109	55
19	Unité 2: L.6, p. 110	19	19	Unité 2: L.6, p. 110	56
20	Unité 2: L.7, p. 120	20	20	Unité 2: L.7, p. 120	56
21	Unité 2: L.8, p. 128	21	21	Unité 2: L.8, p. 128	57
22	Unité 3: L.9, p. 144	22	22	Unité 3: L.9, p. 144	57
23	Unité 3: L.9, p. 146	23	23	Unité 3: L.9, p. 146	58
24	Unité 3: L.9, p. 148	24	24	Unité 3: L.9, p. 148	58
25	Unité 3: L.11, p. 167	25	25	Unité 3: L.11, p. 167	59
26	Unité 3: L.12, p. 176	26	26	Unité 3: L.12, p. 176	59
27	Unité 3: L.12, p. 178, 179	27	27	Unité 3: L.12, p. 178, 179	60
28	Unité 4: L.14, 15, p. 205, 220	28	28	Unité 4: L.14, p. 205, 220	60
29	Unité 4: L.16, p. 225, 226	29	29	Unité 4: L.16, p. 225, 226	61
30	Unité 5: L.17, p. 256	30	30	Unité 5: L.17, p. 256	61
31	Unité 5: L.17, p. 258	31	31	Unité 5: L.17, p. 258	62
32	Unité 5: L.18, p. 265, 269	32	32	Unité 5: L.18, p. 265, 269	62
33	Unité 5: L.19, p. 276, 278	33	33	Unité 5: L.19, p. 276, 278	63
34	Unité 5: L.19, p. 280, 284	34	34	Unité 5: L.19, p. 280, 284	63
35	Unité 6: L.21, p. 300	35	35	Unité 6: L.21, p. 300	64
36	Unité 6: L.21, p. 301	36	36	Unité 6: L.21, p. 301	64
37	Unité 6: L.21, p. 302, 303	37	37	Unité 6: L.21, p. 302, 303	65
38	Unité 6: L.23, p. 321	38	38	Unité 6: L.23, p. 321	65
39	Unité 7: L.25, p. 346, 347	39	39	Unité 7: L.25, p. 346, 347	66
40	Unité 7: L.25, p. 348, 349	40	40	Unité 7: L.25, p. 348, 349	66
41	Unité 7: L.25, p. 349	41	41	Unité 7: L.25, p. 349	67
42	Unité 7: L.26, p. 356	42	42	Unité 7: L.26, p. 356	67
43	Unité 7: L.26, p. 356, 357	43	43	Unité 7: L.26, p. 356, 357	68
44	Unité 7: L.27, p. 365, 367	44	44	Unité 7: L.27, p. 365, 367	68
45	Unité 8: L.29, p. 406	45	45	Unité 8: L.29, p. 406	69
46	Unité 8: L.30, p. 414	46	46	Unité 8: L.30, p. 414	69

Vocabulaire: La vie scolaire

PUZZLE 1: Reprise, page 5

ACROSS

3. Chemistry
5. Art, Drawing
7. Biology
9. Physics
10. French
11. class
13. Civics
17. German
18. senior high school
20. public school
22. private school
24. Spanish
25. Computer Science

DOWN

1. History
2. Physical Education
4. Music
6. Math
8. Economics
12. Languages
14. junior high school
15. Science
16. Geography
19. English
21. Sports
23. class, course

How to talk about things

PUZZLE 2: Reprise, page 13

ACROSS

2. This (here) is . . .
5. What's that? What is it? (6 w.)
9. There is/are . . .

DOWN

1. What is there . . . ? (7 w.)
3. There is (are) no . . . ? (5 w.)
4. Is (Are) there . . . ? (6 w.)
6. That is . . . (2 w.)
7. Those are . . . (2 w.)
8. There is (are) . . . (3 w.)

How to indicate where things are located

PUZZLE 3: Reprise, page 15

ACROSS

   3. to the left of (3 w.)
   5. on
   7. to the right of (3 w.)
   8. under
  10. behind
  11. far from (2 w.)

DOWN

   1. in
   2. next to (3 w.)
   4. between
   6. near (2 w.)
   9. in front of

How to ask for information

PUZZLE 4: Reprise, page 21

ACROSS

2. Who(m)?
3. With whom? (2 w.)
6. At what time? (3. w)
7. When?
8. How?

DOWN

1. Where?
2. What? (4 w.)
4. Why?
5. About what? (2 w.)
6. To whom? (2 w.)

Vocabulaire: La nationalité

PUZZLE 5: Unité 1, Leçon 1, page 33

ACROSS

1. Mexican (f.)
4. Belgian (m./f.)
6. Vietnamese (m.)
8. German (f.)
10. Chinese (m.)
15. Puerto Rican (m.)
17. Canadian (m.)
19. Italian (f.)
20. Korean (f.)

DOWN

2. Egyptian (m.)
3. American (m.)
5. Indian (f.)
7. Cambodian (m.)
9. Russian (m./f.)
10. Cuban (m.)
11. Swiss (m./f.)
12. Japanese (f.)
13. French (m.)
14. English (f.)
16. Israeli (m.)
18. Spanish (m.)

Nom _____

Classe _____ Date _____

Vocabulaire: Les gens – La famille

PUZZLE 6: Unité 1, Leçon 1, page 34

ACROSS

1. grandfather (2 w.)
2. stepsister (2 w.)
6. stepfather (2 w.)
8. niece
10. stepmother (2 w.)
11. granddaughter (2 w.)
15. sister
16. mother

17. cousin (f.)
20. wife
21. daughter
22. cousin (m.)

DOWN

1. grandmother (2 w.)
3. husband
4. uncle
5. grandson (2w.)
7. parent, relative
9. father
12. child
13. aunt

14. family
18. stepbrother (2 w.)
19. nephew
20. son

DISCOVERING FRENCH–BLANC

Vocabulaire: Les gens – Les amis

PUZZLE 7: Unité 1, Leçon 1, page 34

ACROSS

1. classmate (m./f.)
4. best (f.)
6. neighbor (f.)
7. friend (m.)
8. neighbor (m.)

DOWN

1. pal (m.)
2. people
3. person
4. best (m.)
5. pal (f.)
7. friend (f.)

Quelques professions

PUZZLE 8: Unité 1, Leçon 1, page 37

ACROSS

6. fashion model
7. pharmacist (m.)
8. nurse (m.)
13. technician (m.)
15. office worker (m.) (3w.)
18. boss (m.)
19. engineer
20. lawyer (m.)
21. businessperson (m.)
22. computer specialist (m.)
23. dentist (m./f.)

DOWN

1. salesperson (m.)
2. journalist (m./f.)
3. doctor
4. designer, draftsperson (m.)
5. accountant (m./f.)
9. filmmaker (m./f.)
10. doctor
11. actor (m.)
12. photographer
14. writer
16. programmer (m.)
17. secretary

Les expressions avec *être*

PUZZLE 9: Unité 1, Leçon 1, page 44

ACROSS

1. to be currently doing (4 w.)
2. to be early (3 w.)
4. to be late (3 w.)
5. to be on time (4 w.)

DOWN

1. to belong to . . . (2 w.)
3. to agree (3 w.)

Adjectives that come *before* the noun

PUZZLE 10: Unité 1, Leçon 2, page 46

ACROSS

5. new (f.)
7. pretty (m.)
9. old (m.)
10. small (m.)
11. beautiful (f.)
12. bad (m.)

DOWN

1. good (f.)
2. big (m.)
3. young
4. new (m.)
6. old (f.)
8. beautiful (m.)
11. good (m.)

Nom _____

Classe _____ Date _____

Vocabulaire: Quelques descriptions

PUZZLE 11: Unité 1, Leçon 2, page 47a

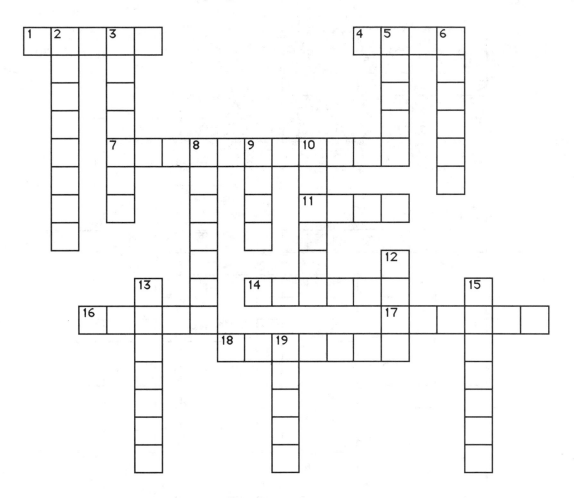

ACROSS

1. rather, enough
4. too, too much
7. nice
11. polite (m.)
14. sad
16. funny
17. shy
18. unfair

DOWN

2. sensitive
3. selfish
5. rich
6. poor
8. boring
9. very
10. impolite (m.)
12. dumb, silly

13. happy (m.)
15. pleasant, nice
19. fair

Encore des adjectifs

PUZZLE 12: Unité 1, Leçon 2, page 47b

ACROSS

1. patient (m.)
3. spontaneous
5. amusing (m.)
6. impatient (m.)
7. intelligent (m.)
9. honest
11. indifferent (m.)
14. competent, capable (m.)
15. sincere
16. strict (m.)
18. harsh
19. distant (m.)
20. dishonest

DOWN

1. pessimistic
2. dynamic
4. organized
8. tolerant
10. optimistic
11. interesting
12. idealistic
13. efficient
17. reserved

Vocabulaire: La personnalité

PUZZLE 13: Unité 1, Leçon 2, page 48

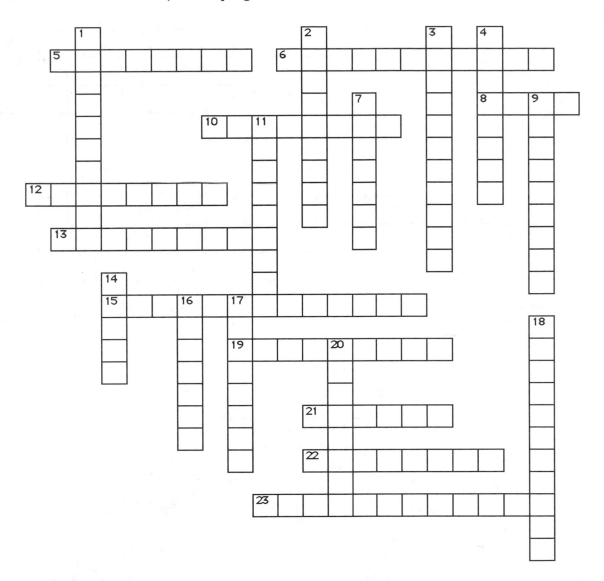

ACROSS

5. curious (f.)
6. imaginative (f.)
8. naive (m.)
10. punctual (m.)
12. boring (m.)
13. generous (f.)

15. conscientious (m.)
19. lazy (m.)
21. cute (m.)
22. musical (m.)
23. intellectual (m.)

DOWN

1. musical (f.)
2. ambitious (m.)
3. unhappy (f.)
4. cute (f.)
7. happy (m.)
9. intuitive (f.)

11. natural (f.)
14. active (m.)
16. athletic (m.)
17. impulsive (m.)
18. witty (f.)
20. serious (f.)

Les expressions avec *avoir*

PUZZLE 14: Unité 1, Leçon 3, page 56

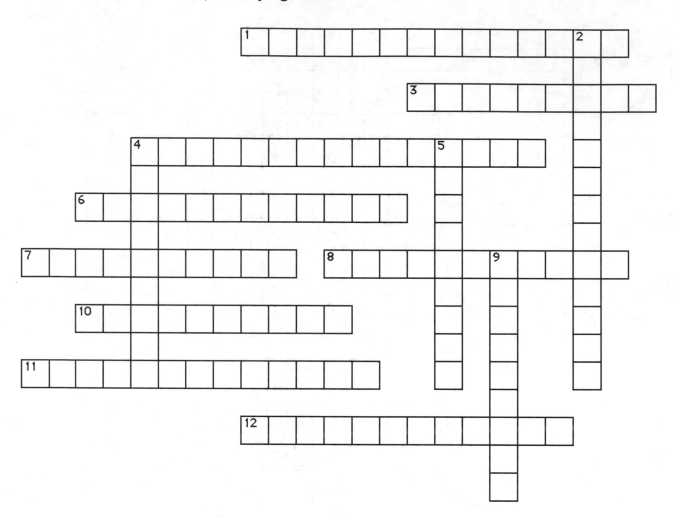

ACROSS

1. What's wrong (with you)? (6 w.)
3. to be thirsty (2 w.)
4. to be lucky (4 w.)
6. to feel like, to want (3 w.)
7. to be cold (2 w.)
8. to be right (2 w.)
10. to be hot (2 w.)
11. What's the matter? (7w.)
12. to be sleepy (2 w.)

DOWN

2. to need (3 w.)
4. to be wrong (2 w.)
5. to be hungry (2 w.)
9. to be afraid (2 w.)

Les expressions avec *faire*

PUZZLE 15: Unité 1, Leçon 3, page 58

ACROSS

4. to do the (food) shopping (3 w.)
5. to go for a walk, ride (3 w.)
6. to cook (3 w.)

DOWN

1. to do the dishes (3 w.)
2. to pay attention (2 w.)
3. to do one's homework (3 w.)

Nom _____

Classe _____ Date _____

Activités du weekend

PUZZLE 16: Unité 2, Leçon 5, page 96

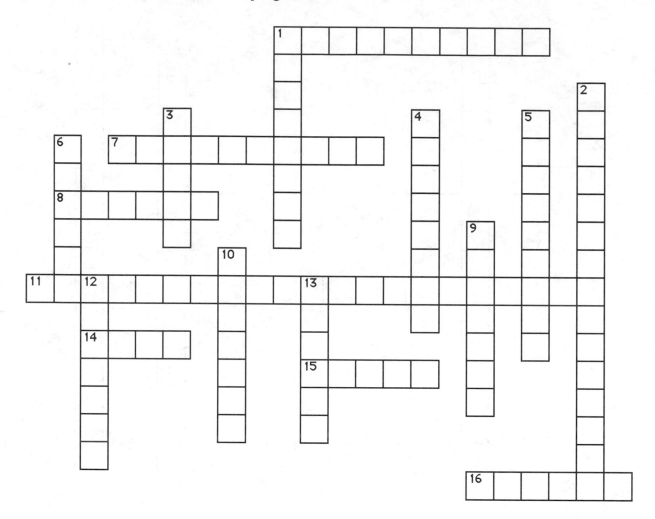

ACROSS

1. to the swimming pool (3 w.)
7. to work
8. to pick up, tidy
11. to take a sunbath (5 w.)
14. to see
15. to help
16. to the movies (2 w.)

DOWN

1. to the beach (3 w.)
2. to stay home (4 w.)
3. to wash
4. to clean
5. to attend (2 w.)
6. to go out
9. to get a tan

10. to the stadium (2 w.)
12. downtown (2 w.)
13. to the café (2 w.)

Vocabulaire: À la campagne

PUZZLE 17: Unité 2, Leçon 5, page 100

ACROSS	**DOWN**	
2. lake	1. plant	14. farm
9. squirrel	3. horse	15. river
10. rabbit	4. hen	16. cow
11. tree	5. leaf	
13. forest	6. bird	
14. flower	7. meadow	
17. field	8. duck	
18. pig	12. fish	

Vocabulaire: Quand?

PUZZLE 18: Unité 2, Leçon 6, page 106

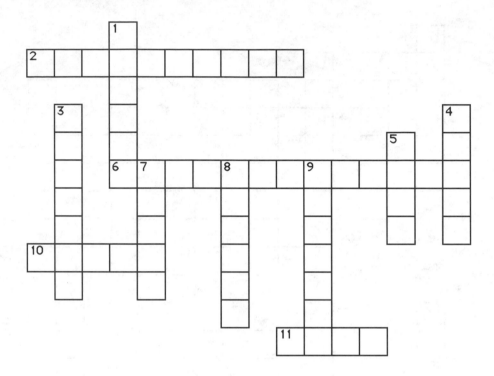

ACROSS

2. finally
6. last Saturday (2 w.)
10. at last
11. ever, already

DOWN

1. never
3. during
4. after
5. yesterday
7. before
8. first (2 w.)
9. then

Les verbes *prendre et mettre*

PUZZLE 19: Unité 2, Leçon 6, page 110

ACROSS

2. to understand (*On*)
5. to allow, to let (*Je*)
6. to take (*Tu*)
8. to understand (*Ils*)
12. to allow, to let (*Elles*)
13. to put (*Vous*)
14. to put (*Nous*)

DOWN

1. to learn (*Nous*)
3. to learn
4. to understand
6. to promise
7. to allow, to let
9. to take (*Vous*)
10. to promise (*Elle*)
11. to put (*Tu*)

DISCOVERING FRENCH–*BLANC*

Vocabulaire: Quelques expressions de temps

PUZZLE 20: Unité 2, Leçon 7, page 120

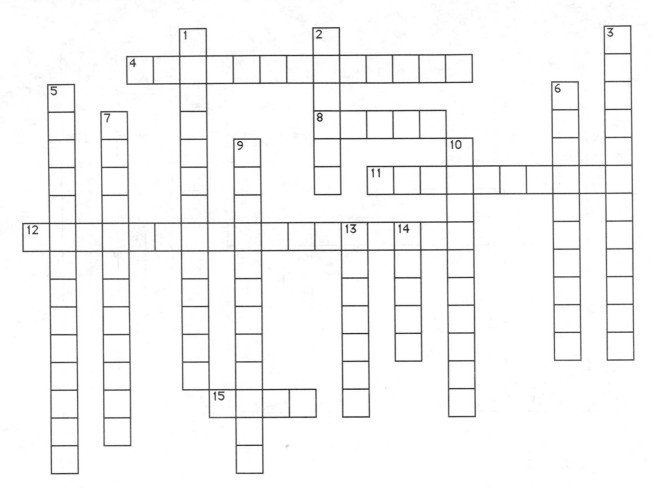

ACROSS

4. yesterday afternoon (3 w.)
8. after
11. tomorrow night (2 w.)
12. next weekend (3 w.)
15. yesterday

DOWN

1. last month (3 w.)
2. tomorrow
3. next summer (3 w.)
5. last year (3 w.)
6. today (2 w.)
7. this week (2 w.)
9. last Monday (2 w.)
10. now
13. this morning
14. before

Les verbes conjugués avec *être*

PUZZLE 21: Unité 2, Leçon 8, page 128

ACROSS

1. to fall
4. to come
7. to go down
10. to come back
11. to return, go home
12. to go out, get out
13. to arrive

DOWN

2. to go up, to get on
3. to pass, go by
5. to go
6. to leave
7. to become
8. to enter, come in
9. to stay

Nom _____

Classe _____ Date _____

Les repas

PUZZLE 22: Unité 3, Leçon 9, page 144

ACROSS

3. knife
7. kitchen
10. to have breakfast (4 w.)
13. dinner, to have dinner
15. cup
16. glass
17. spoon

DOWN

1. plate
2. breakfast (2 w.)
4. food
5. to set the table (3 w.)
6. cafeteria
8. fork
9. napkin

11. table
12. meal
14. lunch, to have lunch

Au café

PUZZLE 23: Unité 3, Leçon 9, page 146

ACROSS

1. steak with French fries (2 w.)
3. mushrooms
5. grilled ham and cheese sandwich (2 w.)
7. ice cream
9. omelet
10. yogurt
14. mineral water (2 w.)
16. anchovies

DOWN

1. salami
2. lemon soda
4. cheese
5. cocoa, hot chocolate
6. carbonated soft drink
8. iced tea (2 w.)
11. tea
12. ham
13. dish
15. beverage

Les plats

PUZZLE 24: Unité 3, Leçon 9, page 148

ACROSS

2. pepper
6. apple juice (3 w.)
7. chicken
10. mustard
13. dessert
16. appetizers (3 w.)
19. sugar
25. grape juice (3 w.)
27. French fries
28. bread
29. milk
30. soup
32. salad

DOWN

1. sole
3. water
4. cereal
5. orange juice (3 w.)
8. veal
9. cake
11. tuna
12. rice
14. fish
15. meat
17. egg
18. salmon
20. jam
21. butter
22. roast beef (2 w.)
23. pie
24. melon
26. salt
31. pork

Quelques verbes

PUZZLE 25: Unité 3, Leçon 11, page 167

ACROSS

1. to drink (*Vous*)
4. to drink (past participle)
5. to clean
7. to send
9. to drink
10. to pay
11. to drink (*Je*)
12. to buy

DOWN

1. to drink (*Nous*)
2. to bring (someone)
3. to prefer
4. to drink (*Ils/Elles*)
6. to drink (*Tu*)
8. to hope
9. to drink (*Il/Elle*)

DISCOVERING
FRENCH–*BLANC*

Les quantités

PUZZLE 26: Unité 3, Leçon 12, page 176

ACROSS

3. jar
6. bottle
8. bag
9. dozen
10. slice

DOWN

1. metric pound
2. box, can
3. pack, package
4. piece
5. kilo(gram)
7. liter

DISCOVERING
FRENCH–BLANC

Expressions de quantité avec *de* + *d'autres* expressions de quantité

PUZZLE 27: Unité 3, Leçon 12, pages 178, 179

ACROSS

4. another (m.) (2 w.)
5. a lot, much, very much (2 w.)
7. a little bit of (3 w.)
9. enough (2 w.)
11. too much, too many (2 w.)

DOWN

1. how much, how many? (2 w.)
2. several
3. some, a few
6. little, few (2 w.)
8. another (f.) (2 w.)
10. other (2 w.)

Rapports et services personnels (L. 14) + quelques verbes (L. 15)

PUZZLE 28: Unité 4, Leçons 14, 15, pages 205, 220

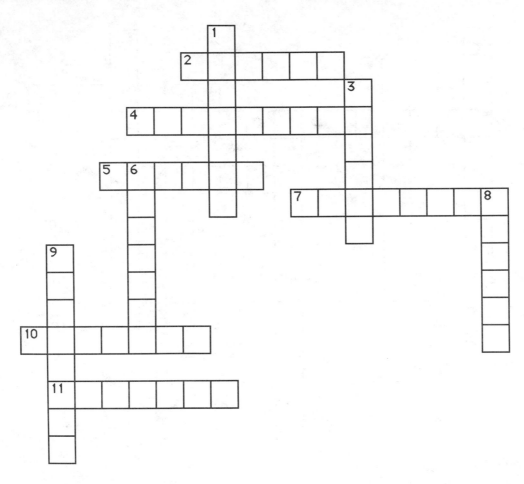

ACROSS

2. to keep
4. to introduce . . . to (à)
5. to give . . . to (à)
7. to look for
10. to show . . . to (à)
11. to find

DOWN

1. to leave
3. to lend, loan . . . to (à)
6. to forget
8. to give back . . . to (à)
9. to bring . . . to (à)

On lit, on écrit, on dit + quelques verbes suivis d'un complément indirect

PUZZLE 29: Unité 4, Leçon 16, pages 225, 226

ACROSS

3. to tell or narrate a story
7. to write (to) (à)
8. to visit (à) (2 w.)
10. postcard (2 w.)
12. to show (to) (à)
15. comics (2 w.)
18. poem
19. magazine (m.)
21. to say, tell (to) (à)
22. lie (noun)
23. to borrow from (à)
24. paper, newspaper
25. to speak, talk to (à)

DOWN

1. to lend, loan (to) (à)
2. to read
4. to phone, call (à)
5. magazine (f.)
6. letter
9. card
11. novel
13. truth
14. story, history
16. to ask for (à)
17. to answer (à)
20. to buy for (à)
21. to give (to) (à)

Quelques sports individuels

PUZZLE 30: Unité 5, Leçon 17, page 256

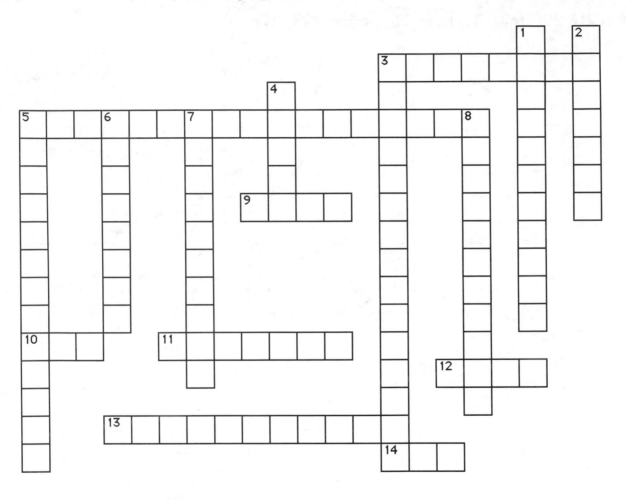

ACROSS

3. skating
5. skate boarding (3 w.)
9. cycling
10. mountain biking
11. jogging
12. surfboarding
13. gymnastics
14. skiing

DOWN

1. hiking (3 w.)
2. aerobics
3. rollerskating (3 w.)
4. sailing
5. windsurfing (3 w.)
6. swimming
7. horseback riding
8. waterskiing (2 w.)

Les parties du corps

PUZZLE 31: Unité 5, Leçon 17, page 258

ACROSS

2. nose
3. arm
4. hair (pl.)
8. neck
9. knee
10. eyes
11. foot
13. ear
15. finger
16. eye (sing.)
18. stomach

DOWN

1. head
3. mouth
4. heart
5. stomach
6. hand
7. face
8. body
12. back
14. shoulder
15. tooth
17. leg

Quelques expressions de temps + pour exprimer son opinion

PUZZLE 32: Unité 5, Leçon 18, pages 265, 269

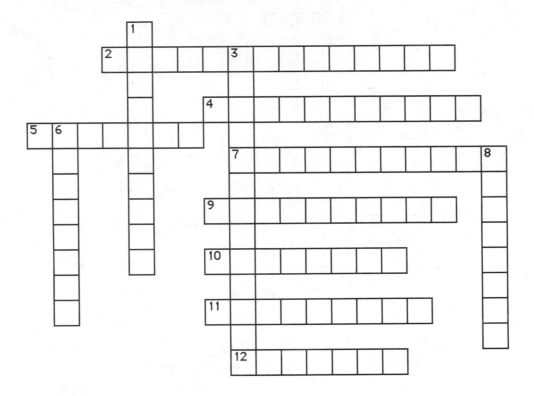

ACROSS

2. from time to time (4 w.)
4. I think that (3 w.)
5. occasionally
7. sometimes
9. I think that (3 w.)
10. seldom, rarely
11. according to me (3 w.)
12. often

DOWN

1. I believe that (3 w.)
3. almost never (2 w.)
6. in my opinion (3 w.)
8. according to me (2 w.)

Les occupations de la journée + la toilette

PUZZLE 33: Unité 5, Leçon 19, pages 276, 278

ACROSS

3. to go to bed (2 w.)
4. shampoo (noun)
6. to comb one's hair (2 w.)
11. hairbrush (3 w.)
13. to brush . . . (2 w.)
15. to get dressed (2 w.)
16. toothpaste
17. to wake up (2 w.)

DOWN

1. to put on make-up (2 w.)
2. to wash up (2 w.)
3. to go for a walk (2 w.)
5. comb (noun)
7. razor
8. to get up (2 w.)
9. to shave (2 w.)
10. lipstick (3 w.)

11. toothbrush (3 w.)
12. soap
14. to rest (2 w.)

How to express yourself when you are in a rush + quelques verbes réfléchis

PUZZLE 34: Unité 5, Leçon 19, pages 280, 284

ACROSS

3. very quickly (3 w.)
8. to apologize (2 w.)
10. to remember (2 w.)
11. to hurry up (2 w.)

DOWN

1. still, always
2. to be in a hurry (2 w.)
4. right away (3 w.)
5. to be ready (2 w.)
6. to have fun (2 w.)
7. not yet, still (2 w.)
9. to stop (2 w.)

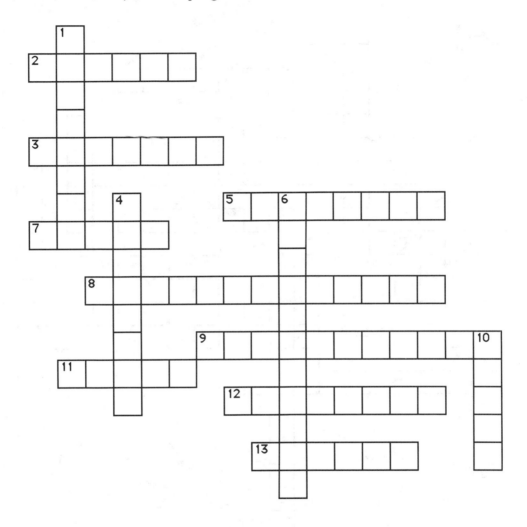 DISCOVERING
FRENCH–*Blanc*

La résidence

PUZZLE 35: Unité 6, Leçon 21, page 300

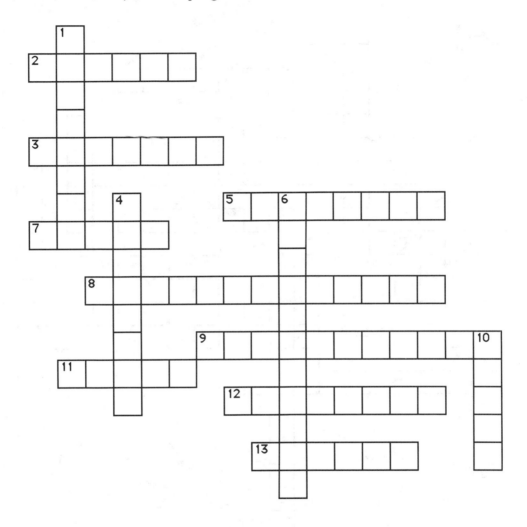

ACROSS

2. house
3. village
5. district, section
7. farm
8. ground floor (3 w.)
9. downtown (m.) (2 w.)
11. town, city
12. countryside
13. old

DOWN

1. suburbs
4. apartment building
6. apartment
10. floor

**DISCOVERING
FRENCH–BLANC**

Les parties de la maison

PUZZLE 36: Unité 6, Leçon 21, page 301

ACROSS

1. ground
2. ceiling
3. window
7. bedroom (3 w.)
10. hall, corridor
11. basement (2 w.)
13. roof
14. informal living room
15. ground floor (3 w.)
17. cellar
19. dining room (3 w.)

DOWN

1. formal living room
2. door
4. garage
5. toilet (pl.)
6. water closet (Brit.)
7. kitchen
8. wall
9. bathroom (3 w.)
12. garden
16. key
18. stair
20. attic

DISCOVERING FRENCH–BLANC

Le mobilier et l'équipement de la maison

PUZZLE 37: Unité 6, Leçon 21, pages 302, 303

ACROSS

2. dishwasher (2 w.)
3. bathtub
8. mirror
12. table
15. microwave (3 w.)
17. chair
19. bookshelf
21. sofa
22. bed
23. lamp
24. sink
25. office, desk
26. toaster (2 w.)

DOWN

1. painting, picture
4. curtains
5. armchair
6. rug, doormat
7. furniture
9. refrigerator
10. cabinets
11. washing machine (3 w.)
13. range, stove
14. oven
16. shower
18. piece of furniture
20. kitchen sink

Quelques expressions de temps

PUZZLE 38: Unité 6, Leçon 23, page 321

ACROSS

2. one evening (2 w.)
3. every day (3 w.)
6. usually (2 w.)
11. usually
13. Tuesday
14. in the evening (2 w.)
16. once (2 w.)
17. several times (2 w.)

DOWN

1. in the past
4. every day (2 w.)
5. on Tuesdays (2 w.)
7. every Tuesday (3 w.)
8. sometimes
9. twice (2 w.)
10. one Tuesday (2 w.)
12. every evening (3 w.)
15. one day (2 w.)

Les vêtements

PUZZLE 39: Unité 7, Leçon 25, pages 346, 347

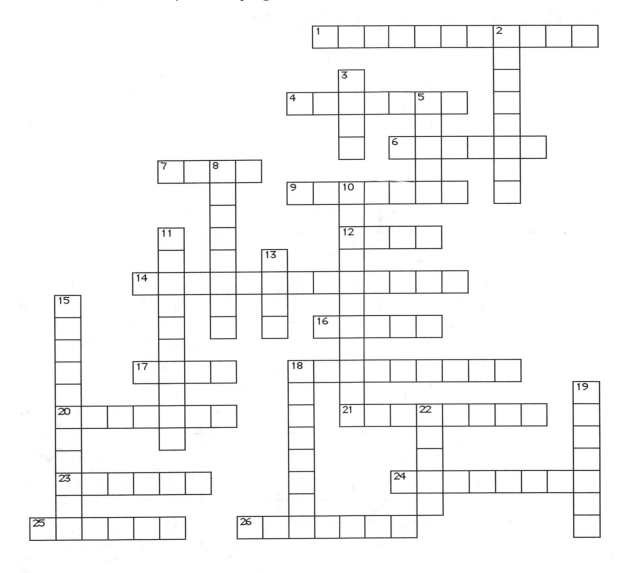

ACROSS

1. socks
4. shirt
6. boots
7. skirt
9. high tops
12. dress
14. bathing suit (3 w.)
16. jacket
17. sweater
18. blouse
20. coat
21. T-shirt
23. blazer
24. sandals
25. sneakers
26. suit

DOWN

2. suit
3. (pair of) jeans
5. shorts
8. pants
10. jogging suit, track suit
11. shoes
13. polo shirt
15. raincoat
18. tights, pantyhose
19. jacket
22. sweatshirt

Nom _____

Classe _____ Date _____

Les accessoires et les articles personnels + les couleurs

PUZZLE 40: Unité 7, Leçon 25, pages 348, 349

ACROSS

3. green
5. light blue (2 w.)
7. bracelet
9. gray
10. gloves
11. pink
16. ring
17. sunglasses (3 w.)
19. black
20. yellow
22. white
24. brown
25. cap
26. wallet
27. red
28. earrings (3 w.)

DOWN

1. tie
2. scarf
3. purple
4. dark blue (2 w.)
6. umbrella
8. chain
12. belt
13. medal
14. beige
15. color
16. blue
18. bag, sack
21. hat
23. necklace

Le dessin + les tissus et les autres matières

PUZZLE 41: Unité 7, Leçon 25, page 349

ACROSS

2. checked (2 w.)
3. striped (2 w.)
4. leather
5. rubber
7. corduroy (2 w.)
11. nylon
12. solid (color)
13. cotton

16. silk
17. flowered (2 w.)
18. fabric
19. canvas, linen
20. pattern, design

DOWN

1. plastic
3. dotted, polka-dotted (2 w.)
6. polyester
7. velvet
8. gold
9. wool
10. fur

14. material
15. silver

Les nombres de 100 à 1 000 000

PUZZLE 42: Unité 7, Leçon 26, page 356

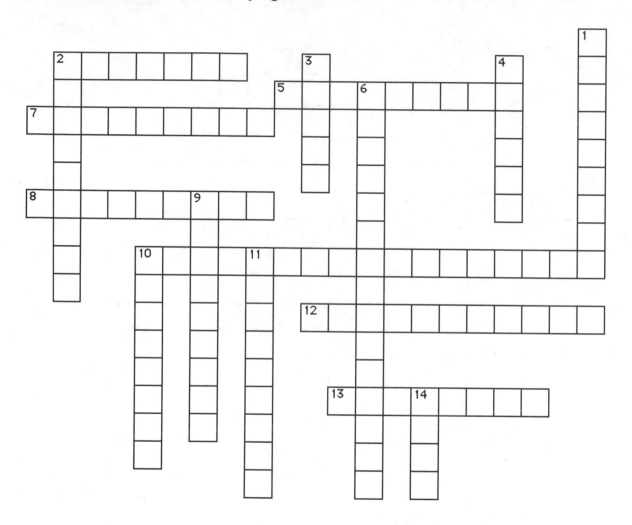

ACROSS

2. 110 (2 w.)
5. 5 000 (2 w.)
7. 1 000 000 (2 w.)
8. 200 (2 w.)
10. 250 (3 w.)
12. 510 (3 w.)
13. 600 (2 w.)

DOWN

1. 2 000 (2 w.)
2. 500 (2 w.)
3. 1 000
4. 101 (2 w.)
6. 420 (3 w.)
9. 900 (2 w.)
10. 10 000 (2 w.)
11. 100 000 (2 w.)
14. 100

Les nombres ordinaux
+ Révision: Les adjectifs irréguliers

PUZZLE 43: Unité 7, Leçon 26, pages 356, 357

ACROSS

3. careful (m.)
5. expensive (m.)
6. good (m.)
8. normal (pl.)
11. Canadian (f.)
16. first (m.)
17. expensive (f.)
18. discreet (f.)
19. discreet (m.)
20. natural (f.)
21. hundredth
22. first (f.)

DOWN

1. natural (m.)
2. generous (m.)
4. generous (f.)
6. good (f.)
7. careful (f.)
9. eleventh
10. fifth
11. Canadian (m.)
12. second
13. normal (sing.)
14. third
15. ninth

DISCOVERING
FRENCH–BLANC

Quelques adjectifs + quelques adverbes

PUZZLE 44: Unité 7, Leçon 27, pages 365, 367

ACROSS

1. slow
2. weak
3. useless
6. nice (f.)
8. easy
11. inexpensive (2 w.)
13. early
15. nice (m.)
18. fast
19. difficult
21. cold

DOWN

1. slowly
4. (for) a long time
5. mean, nasty
7. fast
9. heavy
10. useful
12. expensive
14. warm, hot
16. late
17. light
20. strong

Un peu de géographie

PUZZLE 45: Unité 8, Leçon 29, page 406

ACROSS

4. England
5. Germany
9. China
10. state
11. Cambodia
12. Argentina
15. Portugal
17. Russia
18. Senegal
19. Northeast (2 w.)
21. to spend some time (3 w.)
28. Mexico
29. Ireland
31. Belgium
32. East
34. Australia
37. South
38. Egypt
39. Switzerland
40. Guatemala

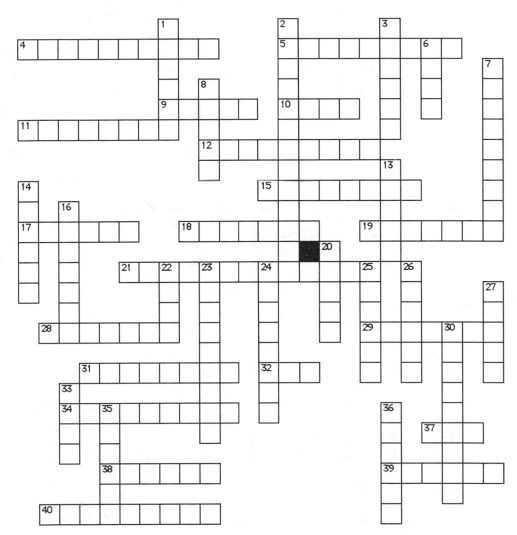

DOWN

1. France
2. to take a trip (3 w.)
3. Canada
6. North
7. continent
8. Lebanon
13. Japan
14. Israel
16. Spain
20. Korea
22. India
23. United States (2 w.)
24. Southwest (2 w.)
25. region
26. Italy
27. West
30. Northwest (2 w.)
33. country
35. Southeast (2 w.)
36. Brazil

Verbes suivis de l'infinitif

PUZZLE 46: Unité 8, Leçon 30, page 414

ACROSS

2. to learn (how) to (2 w.)
4. to decide to (2 w.)
7. to forget to (2 w.)
8. to accept, to agree to (2 w.)
12. to finish (2 w.)

DOWN

1. to hesitate (2 w.)
3. to dream about (2 w.)
5. to try to (2 w.)
6. to continue, go on (2 w.)
8. to stop (2 w.)
9. to begin to (2 w.)

10. to refuse to (2 w.)
11. to stop, quit (2 w.)
13. to succeed in, manage (2 w.)

Answer Key

PUZZLE 1: Vocabulaire: La vie scolaire

Page 1

PUZZLE 2: How to talk about things

Page 2

Answer Key

PUZZLE 3: How to indicate where things are located

Page 3

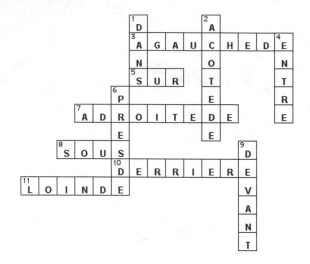

PUZZLE 4: How to ask for information

Page 4

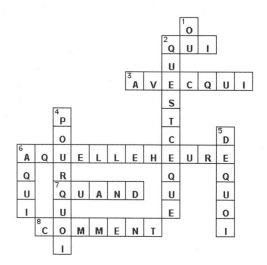

PUZZLE 5: Vocabulaire: La nationalité

Page 5

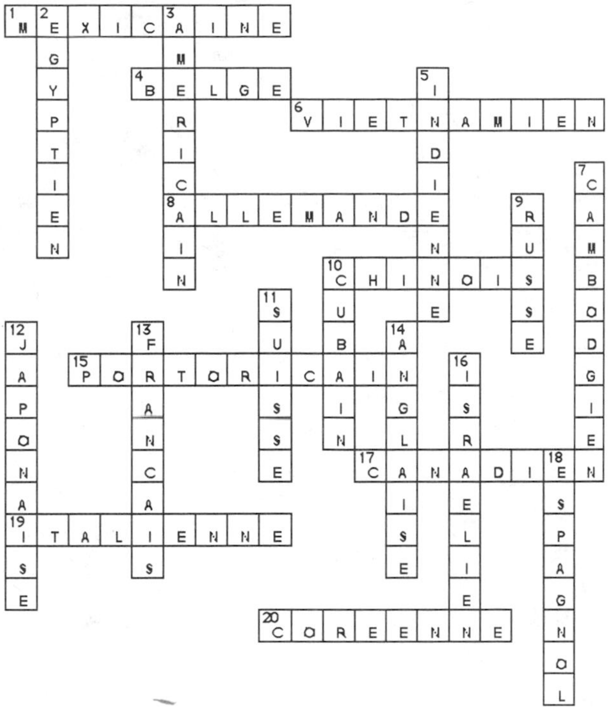
1 MEXICAINE
2 EGYPTIEN
3 AMERICAIN
4 BELGE
5 INDIENNE
6 VIETNAMIEN
7 CAMBODGIEN
8 ALLEMANDE
9 RUSSE
10 CHINOIS
CUBAIN
11 SUISSE
12 JAPONAISE
13 FRANCAIS
14 ANGLAISE
15 PORTORICAIN
16 ISRAELIEN
17 CANADIEN
18 ESPAGNOL
19 ITALIENNE
20 COREENNE

PUZZLE 6: Vocabulaire: Les gens – la famille

Page 6

1 GRANDPERE
GRANDMERE
2 DEMISOEUR
3 MARI
4 ONCLE
5 PETITFILS
6 BEAUPERE
7 PARENT
8 NIECE
9 PERE
10 BELLEMERE
11 PETITEFILLE
12 ENFANT
13 TANTE
14 FAMILLE
15 SOEUR
16 MERE
17 COUSINE
18 DEMIFRERE
19 NEVEU
20 FEMME
FILS
21 FILLE
22 COUSIN

Answer Key

PUZZLE 7: Vocabulaire: Les gens – les amis

Page 7

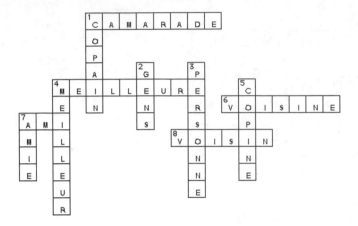

PUZZLE 8: Quelques professions

Page 8

Answer Key

PUZZLE 9: Les expressions avec *être*

Page 9

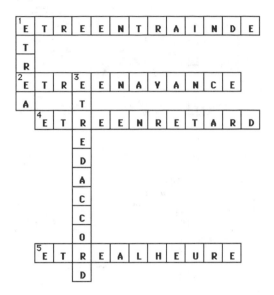

PUZZLE 10: Adjectives that come *before* the noun

Page 10

Answer Key

PUZZLE 11: Vocabulaire: Quelques descriptions

Page 11

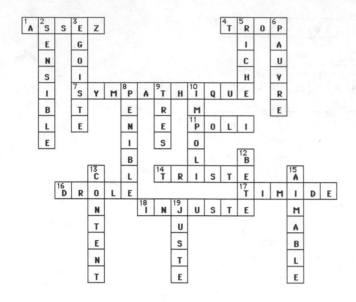

PUZZLE 12: Encore des adjectifs

Page 12

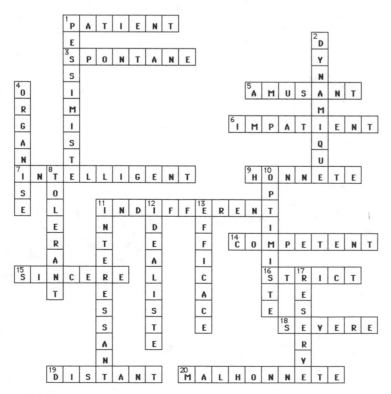

Answer Key

PUZZLE 13: Vocabulaire: La personnalité

Page 13

```
          ¹M              ²A          ³M    ⁴M
    ⁵C U R I E U S E   ⁶I M A G I N A T I V E
      S               B           L     G
      I               I     ⁷H    H   ⁸N A I F  ⁹
      C          ¹⁰P ¹¹O N C T U E L     O       N
      I            A           U    H     N       T
      E            T           R    E     N       U
   ¹²E N N U Y E U X    U           E    R        I
      N            U           U    E     E       T
   ¹³G E N E R E U S E  R           X    U        I
                   E           X         S        V
                ¹⁴A  L                            E
             ¹⁵C O N ¹⁶S ¹⁷C I E N C I E U X
                T    P    M
                I    O ¹⁹P A R E ²⁰S S E U X   ¹⁸S
                F    R    U          E           P
                     T    L          R           I
                     I    S       ²¹M I G N O N   R
                     F    I          E           I
                          F       ²²M U S I C I E N  T
                                     S              U
                               ²³I N T E L L E C T U E L
                                                    L
                                                    E
```

PUZZLE 14: Les expressions avec *avoir*

Page 14

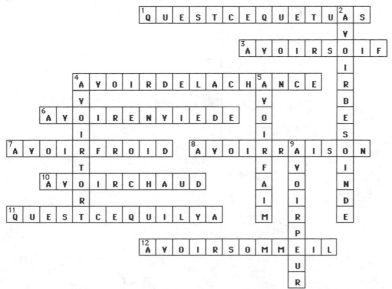

Answer Key

PUZZLE 15: Les expressions avec *faire*

Page 15

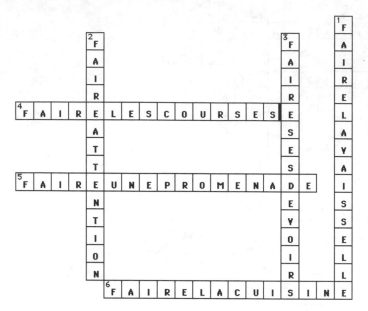

PUZZLE 16: Activités du weekend

Page 16

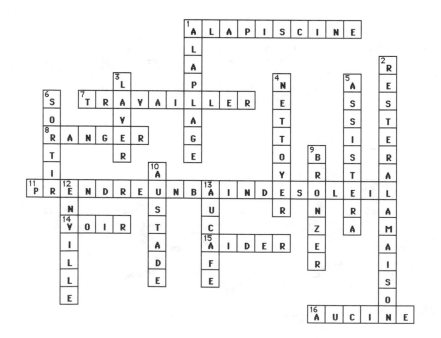

Answer Key

PUZZLE 17: Vocabulaire: À la compagne

Page 17

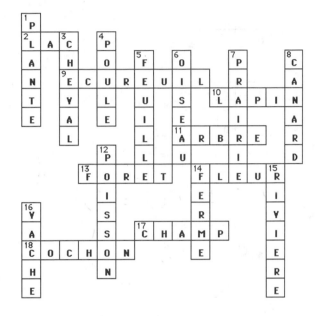

PUZZLE 18: Vocabulaire: Quand?

Page 18

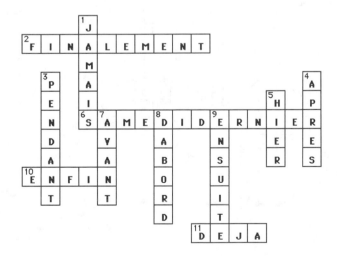

Answer Key

PUZZLE 19: Les verbes *prendre et mettre*

Page 19

Across and down answers:
- COMPREND
- APPRENONS
- PERMETS
- PRENDS
- COMPRENNENT
- COMPRENDRE
- PRENEZ
- PRENNENT
- PERMETTENT
- PROMET
- METTEZ
- METTONS
- PERMETTRE
- PERMETTRE
- APPRENDRE
- MT...

PUZZLE 20: Quelques expressions de temps

Page 20

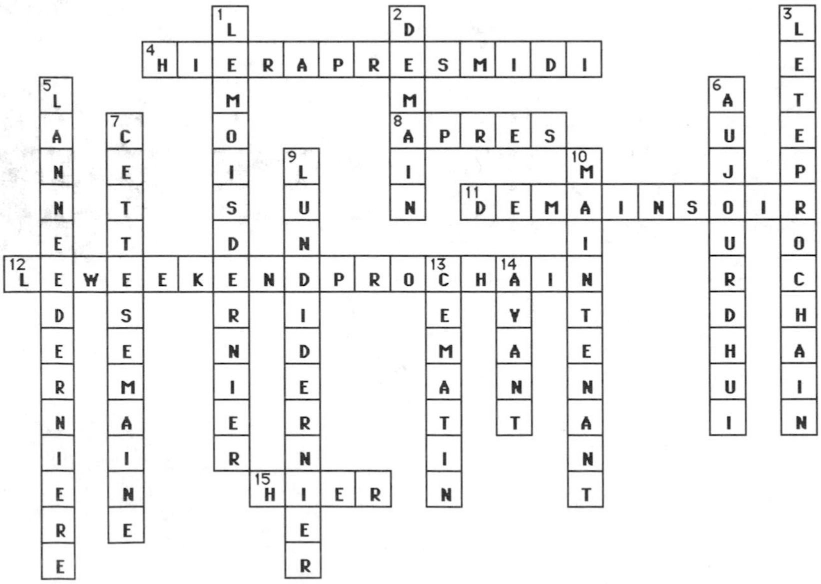

Across:
- 4. HIER APRES MIDI
- 8. APRES
- 11. DEMAIN SOIR
- 12. LE WEEKEND PROCHAIN
- 15. HIER

Down:
- 1. LE MOIS DERNIER
- 2. DEMAIN MATIN
- 3. LE TEPROCHAIN
- 5. L'ANNEE DERNIERE
- 6. AUJOURD'HUI
- 7. CETTE SEMAINE
- 9. LUNDI DERNIER
- 10. MAINTENANT
- 13. CETTE ...
- 14. MAINTENANT

Answer Key

PUZZLE 21: Les verbes conjugués avec être

Page 21

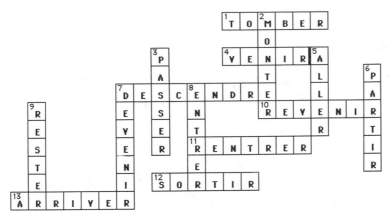

PUZZLE 22: Les repas

Page 22

Answer Key

DISCOVERING FRENCH–BLANC

PUZZLE 23: Au café

Page 23

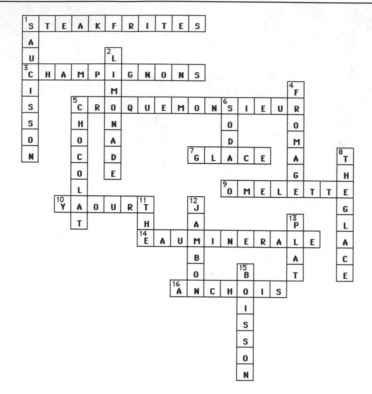

PUZZLE 24: Les plats

Page 24

Answer Key

PUZZLE 25: Quelques verbes

Page 25

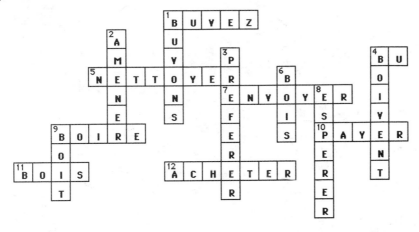

PUZZLE 26: Les quantités

Page 26

Answer Key

PUZZLE 27: Expressions de quantité

Page 27

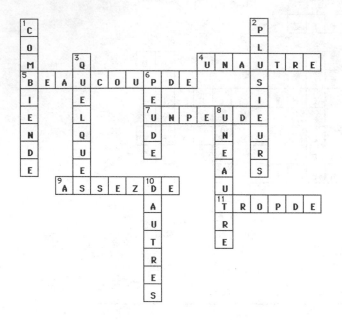

PUZZLE 28: Rapports et services personnels

Page 28

Answer Key

PUZZLE 29: On lit, on écrit, on dit

Page 29

PUZZLE 30: Quelques sports individuels

Page 30

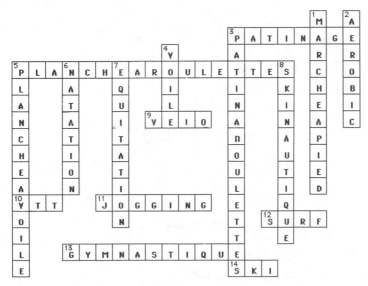

Answer Key

PUZZLE 31: Les parties du corps

Page 31

PUZZLE 32: Quelques expressions de temps + pour exprimer son opinion

Page 32

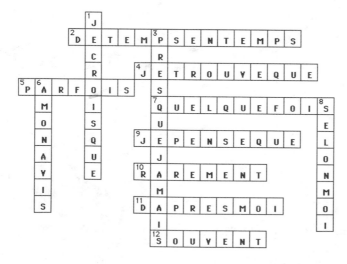

Answer Key

PUZZLE 33: Les occupations de la journée + la toilette

Page 33

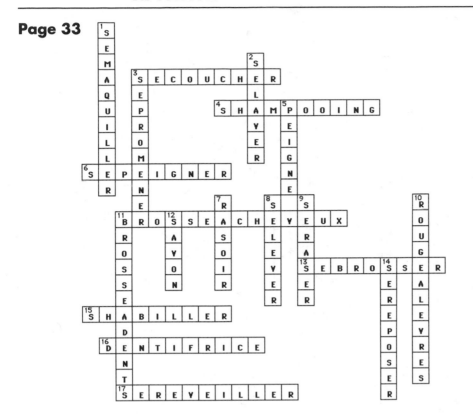

PUZZLE 34: How to express yourself when you are in a rush

Page 34

Answer Key

PUZZLE 35: La résidence

Page 35

PUZZLE 36: Les parties se la maison

Page 36

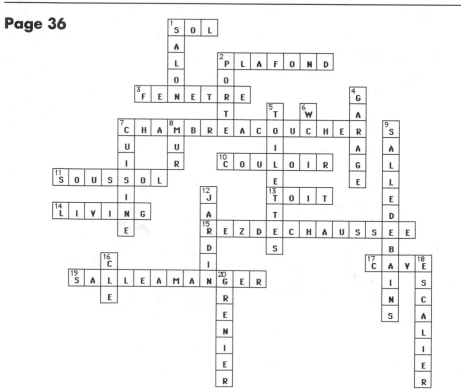

Answer Key

PUZZLE 37: Le mobilier et l'equipement de la maison

Page 37

PUZZLE 38: Quelques expressions de temps

Page 38

Answer Key

PUZZLE 39: Les vêtements

Page 39

PUZZLE 40: Les accessoires et les articles personnels + les couleurs

Page 40

Answer Key

PUZZLE 41: Les dessin + les tissus et les autres matières

Page 41

PUZZLE 42: Les nombres de 100 à 1 000 000

Page 42

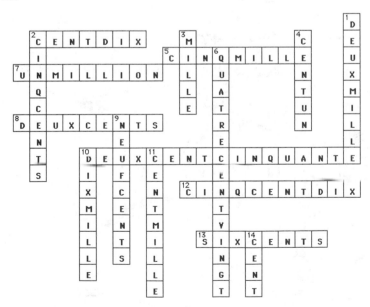

Answer Key

PUZZLE 43: Les nombres ordinaux + Révision: Les adjectifs irréguliers

Page 43

PUZZLE 44: Quelques adjectif + quelques adverbes

Page 44